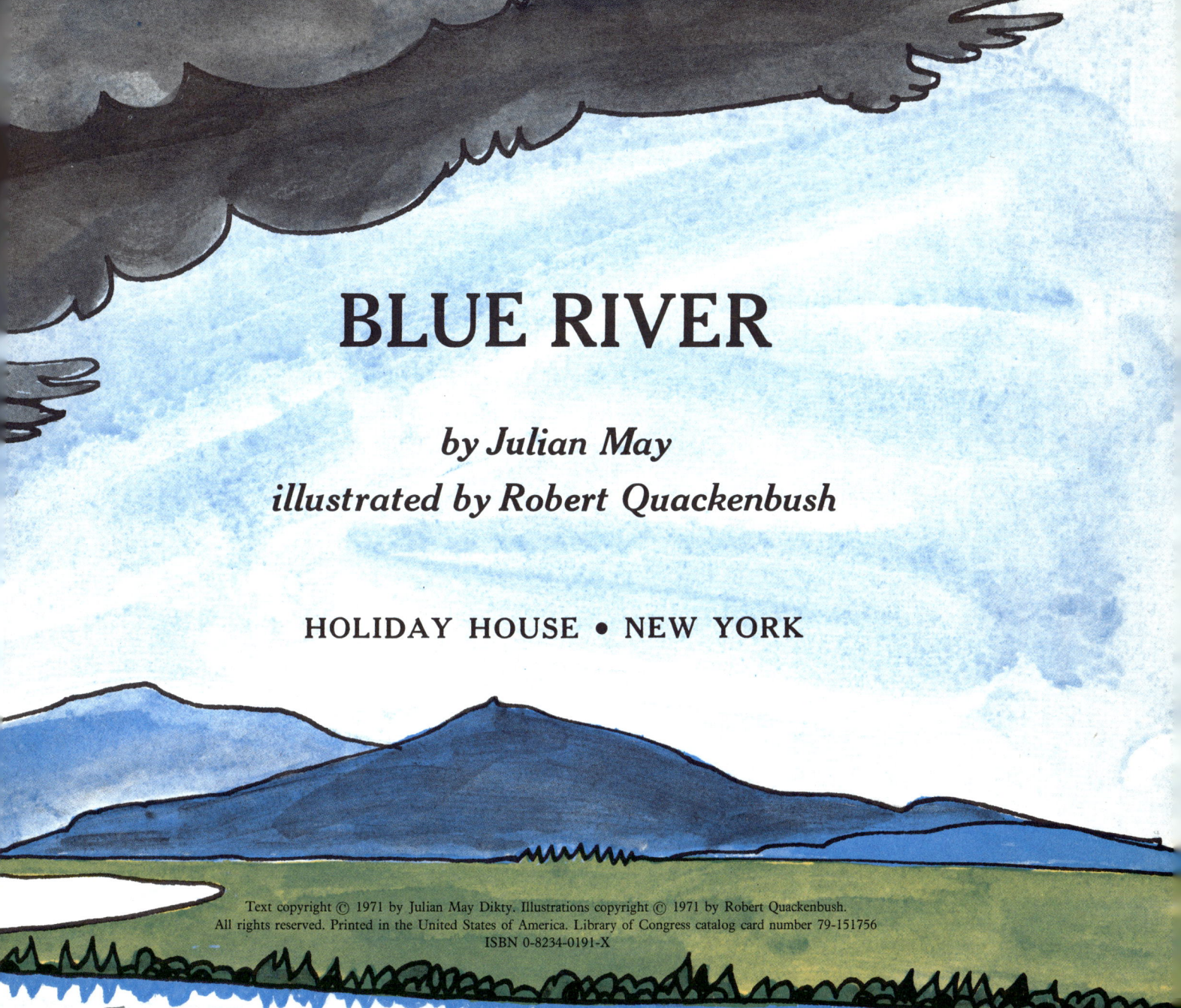

BLUE RIVER

by Julian May

illustrated by Robert Quackenbush

HOLIDAY HOUSE • NEW YORK

Text copyright © 1971 by Julian May Dikty. Illustrations copyright © 1971 by Robert Quackenbush.
All rights reserved. Printed in the United States of America. Library of Congress catalog card number 79-151756
ISBN 0-8234-0191-X

Can we save Blue River?
Once it was clean and beautiful.

Long ago, Indians were the only people in the valley. There were not many of them. They could drink the river water and catch fish of many kinds. Big trees and wild flowers grew about their village.

All kinds of other living things made Blue River their home. Dragonflies laid their eggs in the water. So did frogs. Turtles sunned themselves on the banks. They ate green water plants.

There were quiet pools near the edge of the river. Water birds made their nests there. Mink and otter swam among the reeds. Muskrats built homes there. Other animals came down to the river to drink.

For many years, only Indians lived beside Blue River. But then other people came. They cut down the trees and made farms. One man built a store beside the old Indian village. More people came and built houses.

A town was growing on the banks of Blue River. Lumber for the houses came from a sawmill. Its wheel was pushed by the flowing water.

The Indians went away. So did many of the large wild animals. The river water was still clean enough to drink.

The town grew still larger. People wanted it to be neat and clean. So they threw their garbage into the river. The flowing waters carried it away. Still the town grew. People wanted it to be modern. They built sewers to carry waste from sinks and bathrooms. The sewage poured into the river, and the flowing waters carried it away.

The town became a city. Factories were built. They poured their leftover chemicals into the river. And the flowing waters carried them away.

The river water that flowed into the city was still clean. But the river water that flowed out was full of garbage, sewage germs, and chemicals. It was polluted.

As the polluted waters flowed, they slowly became clean again. Garbage dropped to the bottom. It sank into the mud, or rotted and turned to soil. Sewage germs were killed by sunlight and fresh air.

Many of the chemicals were also changed by the sun, the air, and the water. But the river had to flow for many miles before it was really clean again. And some of the chemicals stayed in the water.

Blue River flowed a long way through the valley. As more years passed, new towns grew all along its banks. They all poured their wastes into the water. And there was more and more pollution.

ALGAE

OSCILLATORIA   NOSTOC   ANABAENA

After a time the water was no longer safe to drink. It had too many sewage germs. Smelly plants called algae filled the water. Only tough fish, such as carp, could live in the dirtiest parts of the river.

Chemicals began killing the insects and useful water plants. Birds no longer built their nests among the smelly pools. Many people were sad about the river. They remembered when it was clean and beautiful.

Newspapers wrote about Blue River. People learned pollution was getting worse. Radio and television programs told everyone the river was dying. Could they save Blue River? It would cost money. It would mean hard work. For a long time, nobody did anything.

Then, one springtime, the river was full of dead fish. "How did this happen?" people asked. A scientist told them. Ice covered the river all that winter. This killed many of the smelly plants. The plants rotted and used up the air in the water. With the air gone, the fish could not breathe.

Finally, the people knew they had to do something.
First, they had to stop dumping garbage into the river.
There are modern ways of getting rid of garbage.

The city had to stop dumping sewage into the river, too. The people would have to build a sewage plant. It would take germs and solid wastes out of the sewer water. Water from the sewage plant would be clean when it flowed into Blue River.

People who cared about the river told what would happen when the sewage was not dumped into the water. The river would be clean again. The smelly plants, the algae, would stop spreading. The fishes and turtles that were still in the river would eat up the algae.

The people still had to ask the factory owners to help—they must stop pouring chemicals into the water. Then the insects would slowly come back to Blue River, and so would the birds and fishes that feed on the insects.

Everyone would have to help, if Blue River was to look the way it once did. The trash along the banks must be picked up. New trees and flowers could be planted to make the riverbank beautiful again.

Can we all work together? Cleaning up the river will take time and money. But if people do not care, the river will die and be lost to us forever. Do we care enough? Can we save Blue River?

AUTHOR'S NOTE

The "Blue River" in this book is a real river that almost died from pollution. It is being saved because of the work of many people. Does a Blue River flow through your city? Will you help to save it?